FUN FALL FOODS
EASY-TO-MAKE SNACKS & TREATS

table of contents

© **Meredith Corporation. For more great ideas, subscribe to** *FamilyFun* **magazine by calling 800-289-4849.**
Published in 2012 by Dalmatian Press, LLC. **Printed in China.**
The DALMATIAN PRESS name is a trademark of Dalmatian Press, Franklin, Tennessee 37067. 1-866-418-2572.

gobble me up

TOTAL TIME: 10 MINUTES | SERVES: 1

Need a snack to put kids in a thankful mood? Here's a healthy option they can have fun making themselves.

YOU WILL NEED

- ❑ Apple
- ❑ Clementine or navel orange
- ❑ Bosc Pear
- ❑ Dried apricot
- ❑ Peanut butter or cream cheese
- ❑ Mini chocolate chips
- ❑ Nut (we used a cashew)
- ❑ Dried cranberry

1. Arrange the apple and clementine or navel orange slices on a plate as shown and lay a cored pear half on top.

2. Use scissors to halve a dried apricot, then snip small triangles from each half and tuck them under the pear to form the feet.

3. Finally, use peanut butter or softened cream cheese to attach mini chocolate chip eyes, a nut beak, and a dried cranberry snood.

pumpkin smoothie

TOTAL TIME: 5 MINUTES | SERVES: 2–3

What can you do when you're in the mood for homemade pumpkin pie, but you're squashed for time? Whip up a batch of these thick and tasty pumpkin smoothies.

YOU WILL NEED

- ❑ ½ cup canned pumpkin
- ❑ ¾ cup milk or vanilla yogurt
- ❑ ¼ teaspoon cinnamon
- ❑ ⅛ teaspoon nutmeg
- ❑ 2 teaspoon brown sugar
- ❑ 4 ice cubes
- ❑ Whipped topping

Combine ingredients in a blender and purée until smooth. Pour the smoothies into small glasses (this drink is rich) and garnish each with a dollop of vanilla yogurt or whipped topping. For a fun touch, add a pinch of cinnamon or a few colored sprinkles.

football fare

TOTAL TIME: 75 MINUTES | SERVES: 4–6

Tackle post-game appetites with a hearty harvest chili (it's made with pumpkin) and sandwich combo.

YOU WILL NEED

FOR PUMPKIN CHILI

- ❑ 2 pounds ground beef or turkey
- ❑ 1 medium onion, chopped
- ❑ 1 cup canned pumpkin
- ❑ 1 (28-ounce) can diced stewed tomatoes
- ❑ 1 (16-ounce) can kidney beans, drained
- ❑ 1 (12-ounce) bottle chili sauce
- ❑ 1 to 2 tablespoons chili powder
- ❑ 2 teaspoons pumpkin pie spice
- ❑ 1 teaspoon brown sugar
- ❑ 1½ teaspoons salt
- ❑ 1 teaspoon pepper

FOR GRILLED CHEESE FOOTBALLS

- ❑ Cheese (your family's favorite)
- ❑ Pumpernickel or wheat bread

1. In a large dutch oven or soup kettle, brown the ground beef or turkey with the onion. Drain any excess grease. Add the remaining ingredients and stir well to mix.

2. Bring to a boil, then reduce the heat and simmer for 1 hour. Ladle into bowls and top with grated cheese, if desired.

3. Warm a lightly greased griddle over medium heat. Sandwich slices of your favorite cheese between pumpernickel or wheat bread. Use a cookie cutter or butter knife to cut the sandwiches into football shapes.

4. Grill the sandwiches on one side until browned. Flip and continue to grill until the other side browns and the cheese begins to melt. Garnish with cheese or mustard "laces" and serve while warm.

pigs in pilgrim hats

TOTAL TIME: 20 MINUTES | **MAKES:** 8 HATS

An old favorite all dressed up for Thanksgiving, these fun bites also make a great party or classroom snack.

YOU WILL NEED

- ❑ 2 to 3 hot dogs
- ❑ Tube of crescent roll dough
- ❑ Bologna (hand-sliced from the deli counter, for a larger diameter)
- ❑ Sliced yellow American or Cheddar cheese
- ❑ Flour

1. Heat the oven to 350°. Cut hot dogs into eight 1-inch segments. Separate the dough along its perforations. On a cookie sheet covered with parchment paper, stand the hot dog segments on end, spaced well apart.

2. Drape a triangle of dough over a segment. Dip a glass in flour, then use it to cut out a circle centered on the hot dog, as shown. With floured hands, press the dough around the segment to form a hat shape. Repeat to make the remaining hats. Bake them for 10 to 12 minutes.

3. Meanwhile, cut eight thin strips of bologna and eight small squares of cheese. Arrange them on the cooled hats as shown (if the ends of the hatband don't meet, use the buckle to cover the gap).

cinnamon cider

TOTAL TIME: 10 MINUTES | **SERVES:** 4-6

Melted cinnamon candies are the secret ingredient in this festive drink.

YOU WILL NEED

- ❑ 1 quart pasteurized apple cider or juice
- ❑ ¼ cup cinnamon-flavor hard candies
- ❑ 1 teaspoon vanilla extract
- ❑ ¼ teaspoon cardamom or cinnamon or ⅛ teaspoon allspice (optional)
- ❑ Cinnamon sticks or orange slices

1. In a medium saucepan, combine the apple cider or juice and candies. Cook the cider over medium heat until the candies dissolve. Stir in the vanilla extract and spice

2. Serve warm in mugs garnished with a cinnamon stick or orange slice.

edible pinecones

TOTAL TIME: 10 MINUTES

These pinecone look-alikes make a tree-mendous snack for your festive gatherings.

Spread a generous amount of cream cheese onto a round cracker. Starting at the bottom, layer almond slices on top of the cream cheese for the scales. Add a small piece of a pretzel stick for the stem and serve with thinly sliced celery pine needles.

mini football subs

TOTAL TIME: 20 MINUTES (after meatballs cook)

You can expect a high number of interceptions when you pass these individual-size meatball sandwiches during halftime festivities.

YOU WILL NEED
- ❏ Meatballs (see recipe below)
- ❏ Spaghetti sauce
- ❏ Shredded Cheese
- ❏ Individual-size rolls

1. First prepare your favorite meatball recipe (or try ours below), shaping each meatball into a mini football before cooking. Once they're cooked, add the meatballs to a skillet of spaghetti sauce and warm them through.

2. For each sub, cut out a V-shaped notch from the top of an individual-size roll, place a meatball in the roll, and top with cheese laces. Finally, get the sandwiches in a huddle on a cookie sheet and place them in a warm oven for a few minutes to melt the cheese.

best homemade meatballs

TOTAL TIME: 45 MINUTES | **MAKES:** 100 MEATBALLS

YOU WILL NEED
- ❏ 1 pound ground beef
- ❏ 1 pound ground turkey
- ❏ 1 pound ground pork
- ❏ 1 (10-ounce) package frozen chopped spinach, thawed, drained, and squeezed dry
- ❏ ½ cup finely grated Parmesan cheese
- ❏ 3 large eggs, beaten
- ❏ 2 tablespoons dried Italian herb seasoning
- ❏ 2 teaspoons garlic powder
- ❏ 2 teaspoons salt
- ❏ 1 teaspoon red pepper flakes
- ❏ ½ cup fine or panko bread crumbs

1. Preheat the oven to 400°. Coat 2 large, rimmed baking sheets with cooking spray.

2. In a large bowl, mix together all the ingredients until well combined. Try not to overmix.

3. Pinch off about a teaspoon of the meat mixture and gently roll it into a 1-inch ball. Repeat, arranging the balls ½ inch apart on the baking sheets. Bake the meatballs until lightly browned and cooked through, 20 to 25 minutes.

fruit gobbler

TOTAL TIME: 20 MINUTES

Whet your family's appetite for the real bird with a fruity tribute. It's easy to assemble—and delicious to take apart!

YOU WILL NEED

- ❏ Bosc pear (head)
- ❏ Melon (body)
- ❏ Cheese (beak and tail feathers)
- ❏ Red bell pepper (snood, feet, and side feathers)
- ❏ Raisins (eyes)
- ❏ Grapes (tail feathers)
- ❏ Bamboo skewers
- ❏ Toothpicks

1. Stabilize the melon body by cutting a thin slice off the rind to form a flat base. Using a section of bamboo skewer, attach a Bosc pear head to the melon, as shown.

2. Cut a cheese triangle beak and red bell pepper snood. Attach both, along with raisin eyes, to the head with sections of toothpicks.

3. Cut red bell pepper feet and set them in place. For tail feathers, skewer cheese cubes and red grapes, then insert the skewers as shown. Pin pepper side feathers in place with toothpicks.

teeny turkeys

TOTAL TIME: 10 MINUTES

Looking for a fun snack that will tide over the kids until the big feast? These bite-size birds are easy for children to make and are sure to be gobbled up.

YOU WILL NEED

- ❏ Cocktail pumpernickel bread
- ❏ Vegetable cream cheese
- ❏ Peas
- ❏ Red bell pepper
- ❏ Pepperoni
- ❏ Cheese
- ❏ Cashew
- ❏ Sliced almonds
- ❏ Parsley
- ❏ Round cookie cutter

1. For each sandwich, spread vegetable cream cheese between 2 slices of cocktail pumpernickel bread.

2. For the head, use a small drinking glass or round cookie cutter to cut a circle from another slice of bread, then adhere it to the top of the sandwich with a dab of cream cheese.

3. Add facial features such as pea eyes, a red bell pepper or pepperoni snood (above the beak), and a pepper, cheese, or cashew beak. Finally, wedge bell pepper strips, sliced almonds, or parsley-sprig feathers between the bread slices.

cupples

TOTAL TIME: 20 MINUTES

Make edible sippers, then fill them with our special holiday concoction or your family's favorite juice.

YOU WILL NEED

FOR EACH CUPPLE	FOR DRINK
❑ Apple	❑ Cranberry juice
❑ Melon baller or spoon	❑ Apple cider
❑ Lemon juice	❑ Seltzer water
	❑ Cinnamon stick

1. To make a cupple, slice off the top of an apple. Hollow it with a melon baller or spoon, leaving ¼-inch-thick walls all around. To prevent browning, brush the cup's edge with lemon juice.

2. Combine 1 part cranberry juice, 1 part apple cider, and 1 part seltzer water. Garnish each drink with a cinnamon stick.

cute cornucopia

This mini horn of plenty guarantees that hungry young guests will have something to nibble on. Set one at each place as a mealstarter, or make a bunch to serve as a kid-friendly hors d'oeuvre platter. To create each cornucopia, cut a **tortilla** in half. Roll it into a cone with the rounded edge at the open end. Secure the cone with a **toothpick**, then fill it with small veggies—we suggest **peas, baby carrots, baby corn ears, grape tomatoes,** and **cornichons (or any small pickle)**. Serve with your favorite dip or dressing.

pilgrim pies

TOTAL TIME: 45 MINUTES | **MAKES:** 10-14 PIES

If you think good old whoopie pies just can't be improved upon, wait until you try these—pumpkin cookies filled with fluffy cream cheese frosting.

YOU WILL NEED

FOR PUMPKIN COOKIES

- ❑ 2 eggs
- ❑ 2 cups light brown sugar
- ❑ 1 cup vegetable oil
- ❑ 1 teaspoon vanilla extract
- ❑ 1 (15-ounce) can pumpkin puree
- ❑ 3 cups flour
- ❑ 1 tablespoon pumpkin pie spice
- ❑ 1 teaspoon baking powder
- ❑ 1 teaspoon baking soda
- ❑ 1 teaspoon salt

FOR CREAM CHEESE FROSTING

- ❑ 4 ounces cream cheese, softened
- ❑ ½ cup butter, softened
- ❑ 2 teaspoons vanilla extract
- ❑ 4 to 5 cups confectioners' sugar

1. Heat the oven to 350°. Beat the eggs, brown sugar, oil, and vanilla extract in a mixing bowl until smooth. Stir in the pumpkin. In a separate bowl, combine the flour, pumpkin spice, baking powder, baking soda, and salt. Add the dry ingredients to the egg mixture a half cup at a time, blending each time until smooth.

2. Drop a heaping tablespoon of batter onto an ungreased cookie sheet, using a moist finger or the back of a spoon to slightly flatten each mound. Bake the cookies for 12 minutes, then transfer them to a wire rack to cool completely.

3. Meanwhile, make the frosting. Beat together the cream cheese, butter, and vanilla extract in a bowl until light and fluffy. Mix in the confectioners' sugar a half cup at a time, until the frosting is spreadable.

4. To assemble the pies, turn half of the cookies bottom side up and spread a generous amount of cream cheese frosting on each one. Top them with the remaining cookies.

aut-yum leaves

TOTAL TIME: 25 MINUTES | MAKES: 3–4 POCKETS

These leaves are filled with chocolate and peanut butter chips, but try jam and cream cheese, or chocolate chips, walnuts, and mini marshmallows, if you prefer.

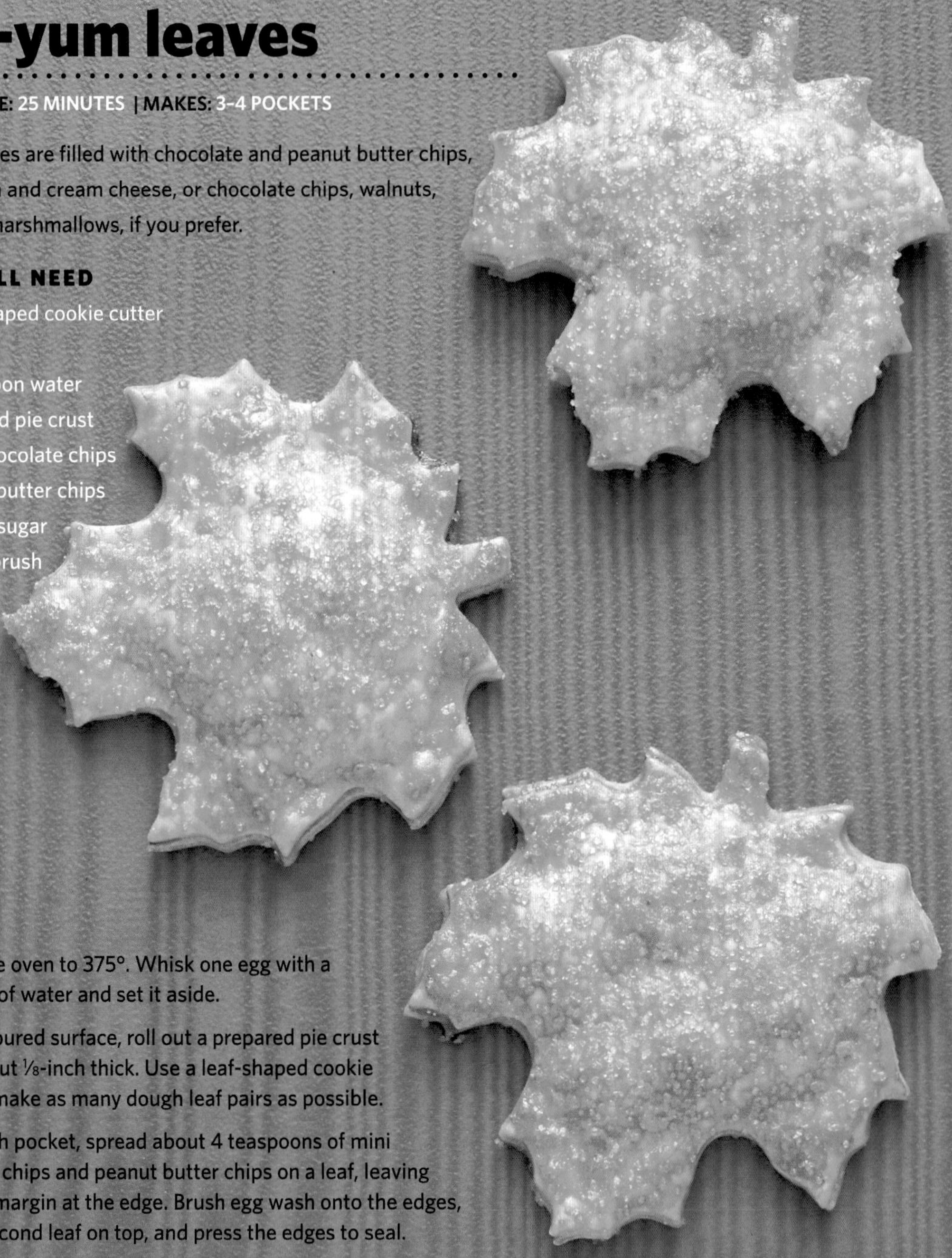

YOU WILL NEED

- Leaf-shaped cookie cutter
- 1 egg
- 1 teaspoon water
- Prepared pie crust
- Mini chocolate chips
- Peanut butter chips
- Coarse sugar
- Pastry brush
- Flour

1. Heat the oven to 375°. Whisk one egg with a teaspoon of water and set it aside.

2. On a floured surface, roll out a prepared pie crust so it's about ⅛-inch thick. Use a leaf-shaped cookie cutter to make as many dough leaf pairs as possible.

3. For each pocket, spread about 4 teaspoons of mini chocolate chips and peanut butter chips on a leaf, leaving a ½-inch margin at the edge. Brush egg wash onto the edges, place a second leaf on top, and press the edges to seal.

4. Brush the top with egg wash and sprinkle it generously with coarse sugar. Bake the leaves on a parchment-covered cookie sheet until their edges are just beginning to brown, about 12 minutes. Let them rest on the sheet a few minutes before moving them to a cooling rack.

marshmallow pilgrim hats

TOTAL TIME: 10 MINUTES | MAKES: 24 HATS

These edible hats are great for classroom parties.

YOU WILL NEED
- ❏ 24 chocolate-striped shortbread cookies
- ❏ 12-ounce package of chocolate chips
- ❏ 24 marshmallows
- ❏ Tube of yellow decorators' frosting

1. Set the chocolate-striped cookies with stripes down on a tray covered with wax paper, spacing them well apart.

2. Melt the chocolate chips in a microwave or double boiler.

3. One at a time, stick a wooden toothpick into a marshmallow, dip the marshmallow into the melted chocolate, and promptly center it atop a cookie.

4. Using a second toothpick to lightly hold down the marshmallow, carefully pull out the first toothpick.

5. Chill the hats until the chocolate sets, then pipe a yellow decorators' frosting buckle on the front of each hat.

edible indian corn

TOTAL TIME: 20 MINUTES | MAKES: 15 TREATS

Ears a fall treat that makes an extra special dessert.

YOU WILL NEED
- ❏ 4 tablespoons butter
- ❏ 4 cups mini marshmallows
- ❏ 5 cups puffed corn cereal
  (we used Kix cereal)
- ❏ 1⅓ cups diced dried fruit (we used raisins, papaya, cranberries, and apricots)
- ❏ Craft sticks
- ❏ Fruit leather (yellow, red, and green)

1. In a large pot, melt butter and mini marshmallows over low heat (about 5 minutes).

2. Remove the mixture from the stove and use a wooden spoon to stir in puffed corn cereal and diced dried fruit. Allow the mixture to cool for about 10 minutes.

3. Using buttered hands, shape each treat by pressing ⅓ cup of the mixture around a craft stick. Add fruit leather husks to the bottom of the ear, slightly moistening them to help them stick if needed.

sweet turkeys

TOTAL TIME: 15 MINUTES (after cupcakes bake)

Candy corn plumage and shortbread wings guarantee that these irresistable treats will be gobbled up as soon as they land on the table.

YOU WILL NEED

- Cupcakes
- Chocolate frosting
- Oval shortbread cookies
- Candy corn pieces
- White frosting
- Black decorators' gel
- Red fruit leather

1. Frost the cupcake, then press in a cookie head and 2 cookie wings.

2. Press in a row or two of candy corn tail feathers.

3. To make an eye, add a small dot of white frosting to the head, then add a dot of black decorators' gel for a pupil.

4. For a beak, cut the white tip from a piece of candy corn and press it into place.

5. To make the wattle, cut a 1-inch square of fruit leather. Roll it into a tube and stick it in place over the beak using a dab of white frosting.

nutty for acorns

TOTAL TIME: 20 MINUTES

Kids are sure to fall for these bite-size sweets, made from mini vanilla wafers and chocolate kisses.

YOU WILL NEED

❑ Chocolate frosting
❑ Mini vanilla wafers
❑ Chocolate kisses
❑ Pretzel sticks

1. For each acorn, use chocolate frosting to attach a mini vanilla wafer to a chocolate kiss.

2. Snap a ¼ -inch section from a pretzel stick for a stem and use frosting to attach it to the wafer. Let the frosting set for 20 minutes before serving.

gobbling-good cupcakes

TOTAL TIME: 15 MINUTES (after cupcakes bake) | **MAKES:** 24 CUPCAKES

If you want to hatch a novel holiday dessert that your kids can help make, these tasty turkeys fit the bill.

YOU WILL NEED

❑ 24 frosted cupcakes
❑ 24 Nutter Butter cookies
❑ White frosting or decorators' gel
❑ Mini chocolate chips
❑ Fruit leather (various colors)
❑ Toothpicks

1. To make each turkey, press the lower portion of a Nutter Butter cookie into a frosted cupcake for the bird's head.

2. Use tiny dabs of frosting to stick on mini-chocolate chip eyes and a red fruit leather wattle.

3. For each turkey's tail, use a butter knife to cut out a dozen feather shapes (about 3 inches long and 1 inch wide) from fruit leather.

4. Lay 6 of the feather shapes on a flat surface and place a wooden toothpick lengthwise atop each so that one end of the toothpick extends about an inch below the feather. Layer another fruit leather feather atop each of the 6 shapes, sandwiching the toothpicks between them.

5. Press the 2 layers together to make them stick, then fringe the edges of the feather with a butter knife. Now your child can stick the colored feathers into the cupcake behind the cookie head.

mini caramel apples

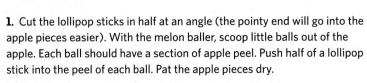

TOTAL TIME: 20 MINUTES

Bite-size versions of the fall fair treat, these tiny "caramel" apples are a great party snack.

YOU WILL NEED

- ❏ 4-inch lollipop sticks
- ❏ Melon baller
- ❏ Granny Smith apples (one apple makes about 8 mini apples)
- ❏ Butterscotch or peanut butter chips
- ❏ Chopped nuts, nonpareils, sprinkles, or shredded coconut (optional)
- ❏ Small paper candy cups

1. Cut the lollipop sticks in half at an angle (the pointy end will go into the apple pieces easier). With the melon baller, scoop little balls out of the apple. Each ball should have a section of apple peel. Push half of a lollipop stick into the peel of each ball. Pat the apple pieces dry.

2. Melt the chips according to the package directions. Dip and swirl the mini apples in the melted chips, then roll the apples in nuts, sprinkles, nonpareils, or coconut, if desired. Place the mini apples in paper candy cups to set.

3. Store in an airtight container.

sweet as pie

TOTAL TIME: 30 MINUTES (after cupcakes bake) | **MAKES:** 12 CUPCAKES

These cute cherry pies have a secret—they're cupcakes in disguise.

YOU WILL NEED

- ❏ 1 dozen of your favorite cupcakes
- ❏ 16-ounce can white frosting
- ❏ 3 drops yellow food coloring
- ❏ 1 teaspoon cocoa powder or 1 tablespoon chocolate syrup
- ❏ Red chocolate candies (we used M&M's)

1. Tint a 16-ounce can of white frosting with 3 drops of yellow food coloring and either 1 teaspoon cocoa powder or 1 tablespoon chocolate syrup, then frost the cupcakes.

2. Transfer the remaining frosting to a ziplock bag, snip off a corner, and set the bag aside. Press red chocolate candies (such as M&M's) onto the top of each cupcake as shown, then use the bagged frosting to pipe a lattice pattern over them and a zigzag crust around the edge.

mini pumpkins

You can harvest a whole pumpkin patch full of these sweet treats in minutes. For each pumpkin, cut one circus peanut in half. Cut a small piece from a green gumdrop and trim away the sugar coating so you have a dot of the sticky inside. Use this piece to adhere the two halves of the circus peanut together, bottom to bottom. Roll the pumpkin in the palms of your hands to make it round. Press lightly; you don't want to compress the candy too much. Use a skewer or toothpick to poke a hole in the top of the pumpkin and draw lines down the sides. Cut another small piece from the green gumdrop and roll it in granulated sugar, molding it into a slightly conical stem shape with your fingers. Insert the stem into the hole on the top of the pumpkin.

easy as pie

TOTAL TIME: 30 MINUTES | **SERVES:** 8

Disguised as a certain pumpkin-flavored dessert, this oversize sugar cookie will add a whimsical touch to your Thanksgiving table.

1. Heat the oven to 350°. Lightly dust a sheet of parchment paper and a rolling pin with flour. On the paper, roll out the dough into a 9½- to 10-inch circle. Place a 9-inch pie pan on top and trim away the dough's edges. Transfer the dough, on the paper, to a cookie sheet and bake it until golden brown, 15 to 20 minutes (do not overbake). Let it cool 1 minute, then carefully transfer it, still on the paper, to a rack to cool completely.

2. Cover the cookie to its edges with the frosting and press the pecan pieces in place to form the crust. Slice the cookie as you would a pie and serve with whipped cream.

YOU WILL NEED

- ⅔ of a 16.5-ounce roll refrigerated sugar cookie dough
- ¾ cup orange frosting
- Pecans, halved crosswise
- Whipped cream

18

acorn dough nuts

Your kids will go nutty for these clever fall treats, which look like acorns but taste a whole lot sweeter.

YOU WILL NEED

❑ Chocolate Frosting or Peanut Butter
❑ Doughnut holes
❑ Crumbled toffee or crushed peanuts
❑ Pretzels

1. Frost about a third of a plain or glazed doughnut hole with chocolate frosting or peanut butter.

2. Roll the frosted top in crumbled toffee (found in the baking section) or crushed peanuts. Add a small piece of a pretzel for the stem.

caramel apple muffins

TOTAL TIME: 30 MINUTES

Inspired by a fall favorite, this fool-the-eye treat makes clever use of an apple muffin and cream cheese frosting.

YOU WILL NEED

❑ Your favorite apple muffins
❑ 8 ounces cream cheese, softened
❑ 2 tablespoons plus 1 teaspoon maple syrup
❑ 1 teaspoon vanilla extract
❑ Orange and brown paste food coloring
❑ Chopped nuts
❑ Craft sticks

1. Bake a batch of your favorite apple muffins in reusable or paper liners and let them cool.

2. Use an electric mixer to blend 8 ounces softened cream cheese, 2 tablespoons plus 1 teaspoon maple syrup, and 1 teaspoon vanilla extract until smooth. Add paste food coloring: 1 small dollop of orange and 2 small dollops of brown. Blend until evenly combined. If needed, add more color until the desired shade of caramel is reached.

3. Frost each muffin and coat it with chopped nuts. Slide a craft stick into the center of each muffin.

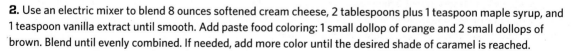

pumpkin meringue pie

TOTAL TIME: 2 HOURS (then cool for 3 hours) | SERVES: 8-10

This recipe will please both pumpkin pie and lemon meringue lovers.

YOU WILL NEED

FOR THE PIE

❏ 9-inch deep-dish piecrust (fresh or frozen)
❏ Aluminum foil
❏ Dry rice or dried beans (or pie weights)
❏ 1 (15-ounce) can solid-pack pumpkin
❏ 1 cup heavy cream
❏ ½ cup whole milk
❏ 2 large eggs
❏ ¾ cup packed light brown sugar
❏ 1 teaspoon cinnamon
❏ 1 teaspoon ginger
❏ ⅛ teaspoon ground cloves
❏ ¼ teaspoon salt

FOR THE MERINGUE

❏ 3 large egg whites, at room temperature
❏ ⅛ teaspoon cream of tartar
❏ ⅓ cup sugar

1. Heat the oven to 400°. Shape the piecrust edge into a high-standing rim. Line the crust with a sheet of aluminum foil, gently pressing it into place. Pour about an inch of dry rice or dried beans onto the foil to weigh it down. Place the crust on the center oven rack and bake it for 15 minutes.

2. Carefully remove the foil and rice or beans by lifting the foil at the edges. Set it aside (the rice or beans can be reused several times). With a fork, prick the bottom of the crust 5 or 6 times to prevent puffing. Lower the heat to 375° and bake the crust 10 minutes more. Transfer it to a wire rack. Reduce the oven temperature to 350°. Note: Frozen crusts do not require foil or weights and should be baked at 400° for 10 minutes total.

3. In a large bowl, whisk together all the filling ingredients until well blended. Set the piecrust on a baking sheet and pour in the filling. Bake the pie until it's puffy around the sides and set in the center, about 50 minutes, then transfer it to a wire rack to cool. Raise the oven temperature to 375°.

4. While the pie cools, make the meringue. In a medium-size bowl, use an electric mixer at medium speed to beat the egg whites until frothy, about 2 minutes. Add the cream of tartar and continue to beat until soft peaks form, about 2 minutes more. Slowly blend in the sugar, then increase the mixer's speed to medium-high and beat the egg whites until they are stiff and glossy, about 2 minutes more.

5. Spoon the meringue onto the pie, then use the back of the spoon to form small peaks. Return the pie to the oven and bake it until the meringue is golden brown, about 10 minutes. Transfer the pie to a wire rack to cool completely.

fruity indian pudding

TOTAL TIME: 2 HOURS | SERVES: 16

Our version of this baked, colonial American dessert contains apples and raisins, combined with the traditional ingredients of cornmeal and molasses.

YOU WILL NEED

- ¼ cup butter
- ¾ cup packed brown sugar
- 6 cups milk
- ⅔ cup yellow cornmeal
- 2 large eggs
- ¼ cup light molasses
- 1½ teaspoons cinnamon
- ½ teaspoon ginger
- 1 teaspoon vanilla extract
- 1 medium apple, peeled, cored, and chopped (we recommend Jonathan, Rome Beauty, or Gala)
- ⅓ cup raisins
- Whipped cream or vanilla ice cream (optional)

1. Heat the oven to 325°. Grease a 9- by 13-inch glass or ceramic baking dish.

2. In a large heavy saucepan or Dutch oven, bring the butter, sugar, and 5 cups of the milk to a simmer over medium heat, stirring to dissolve the sugar and melt the butter, about 5 minutes.

3. In a small bowl, stir together the cornmeal and remaining cup of milk, then whisk it gradually into the heated milk mixture. Cook over medium heat until thickened, whisking frequently to make sure the mixture isn't burning or sticking to the bottom of the pan, about 20 minutes. Remove the pan from the heat.

4. Whisk together the eggs, molasses, cinnamon, and ginger in a medium bowl. Add them to the thickened cornmeal mixture, whisking everything together thoroughly, then stir in the vanilla, apple, and raisins.

5. Transfer the pudding to the prepared dish. Bake until it's golden brown and the center no longer jiggles when the pudding is shaken, about 1½ hours.

6. Serve the pudding, warm or at room temperature, in bowls and topped with whipped cream or ice cream, if you like.

classic bread pudding

Here's something to be thankful for: an irresistible dessert made from a few simple ingredients.

YOU WILL NEED

- ❑ 1 (1-pound) day-old baguette or loaf of Italian bread
- ❑ ½ cup golden raisins
- ❑ 4 large eggs
- ❑ 1 cup whole milk
- ❑ ½ cup plus 2 tablespoons sugar
- ❑ 1 cup whipping cream
- ❑ 1 teaspoon vanilla extract
- ❑ ½ teaspoon cinnamon
- ❑ Whipped cream for serving (optional)

1. Generously coat an 8-inch square baking dish with butter. Remove the crust from the loaf of bread and slice the loaf into 1-inch cubes. Place the cubes in the dish and sprinkle the raisins on top.

2. Whisk the eggs in a large bowl. Add the milk, ½ cup sugar, whipping cream, vanilla extract, and cinnamon. Whisk again until the mixture is well blended.

3. Heat the oven to 350°. Pour the egg mixture over the bread and raisins. Let the ingredients stand for 15 to 20 minutes to allow the bread to absorb the custard. Use a spoon to occasionally push down the bread cubes as they soak.

4. Sprinkle the remaining 2 tablespoons of sugar over the pudding, then place the baking dish in a larger baking or roasting pan. Put the combined pans on the middle rack of the oven, then pour hot water into the larger pan (an adult's job) until it reaches halfway up the sides of the smaller dish.

5. Bake the pudding until it's puffed and golden brown on top and a toothpick inserted into the center comes out clean, 45 to 50 minutes. Remove the pudding from its water bath and set it on a wire rack. Let the dessert cool for 15 minutes before serving, with a dollop of whipped cream if you like.

handprint pumpkin pie

TOTAL TIME: 90 MINUTES | SERVES: 8-10

Let your kids personalize this classic pumpkin pie with a handprint pie-dough turkey.

YOU WILL NEED

- ❏ 1 (15-ounce) package refrigerated piecrust
- ❏ 1 (16-ounce) can packed pumpkin
- ❏ 1 (14-ounce) can sweetened condensed milk
- ❏ 2 eggs
- ❏ 1 teaspoon apple pie spice
- ❏ 1 cup semisweet chocolate chips (optional)

1. Heat the oven to 375°, then make the turkey handprint for the pie. Trace your child's handprint on a piece of lightweight cardboard, then cut it out to create a stencil. Place the stencil over one of the circles of pie dough and cut around it, adding turkey feet to the bottom of the hand.

2. Place the cutout on a nonstick baking sheet. Brush with water and sprinkle lightly with sugar. Bake for 8 to 12 minutes or until golden brown. Let cool.

3. Next, place the remaining circle of pie dough in a 9-inch glass pie pan. Press the crust firmly against the sides and bottom of the pan. Crimp the edges.

4. In a large mixing bowl, combine the pumpkin, sweetened condensed milk, eggs and apple pie spice. Mix until smooth. Stir in the chocolate chips, if desired.

5. Pour the mixture into the piecrust and bake at 375° for 35 to 40 minutes or until an inserted knife comes out clean (except for melted chocolate).

6. Place the baked turkey handprint cutout in the center of the pie and allow the pie to cool before serving.

apple crisp à la mode

TOTAL TIME: 1 HOUR | SERVES: 6

This classic apple dessert, with its crunchy topping, is easier to make than pie and just as tasty!

YOU WILL NEED

- ❏ 6 apples (or 6 cups of apple slices)
- ❏ 1½ cups rolled oats
- ❏ ¾ cup brown sugar
- ❏ ¼ cup all-purpose flour
- ❏ 1 teaspoon cinnamon
- ❏ ¼ teaspoon nutmeg
- ❏ ¼ teaspoon salt
- ❏ ½ cup butter, softened
- ❏ Whipped cream or ice cream

1. Heat oven to 375° and lightly butter an 8- or 9-inch-square baking pan. Peel, core, and slice the apples and arrange them evenly in the prepared pan.

2. Place the oats, brown sugar, flour, spices, and salt in a sealable plastic bag, close, and shake until combined. Cut the softened butter into 1-inch pieces and add to the oat mixture. Close the bag again and knead or squeeze until the mixture holds together.

3. Open the bag and crumble the topping evenly over the apples. Bake the apple crisp for 40 to 45 minutes or until the topping is golden brown and the juices begin to bubble around the edges. Cool slightly, then serve with whipped cream or ice cream.

FamilyFun

Cooking with Kids

FUN FALL FOODS

Apples, pumpkins, and more harvest-season yumminess! The experts at *FamilyFun* magazine share their favorite fall foods and Thanksgiving treats that kids will love to help make—and eat! These recipes are great for holiday get-togethers, classroom snacks, and fun at the Thanksgiving kids' table.

DalmatianPress234020414F16818245-05/12

DPCI: 234-02-0414

$1.00   ISBN 978-1-4530-5799-5

CE15003/0212

9 781453 057995

T2-CBN-816

Distributed by **Dalmatian Press, LLC**
Franklin, TN 37068-2068 • 1-866-418-2572
Printed in Haining, Zhejiang, China